THE
JOURNEY

MAGGIE OGUNBANWO

The Journey
Published in Great Britain in 2023
by Graffeg Limited.

Written by Maggie Ogunbanwo copyright © 2023.
Designed and produced by Graffeg Limited copyright
© 2023.

Graffeg Limited, 24 Stradey Park Business Centre,
Mwrwg Road, Llangennech, Llanelli,
Carmarthenshire, SA14 8YP, Wales, UK.
Tel: 01554 824000. www.graffeg.com.

Maggie Ogunbanwo is hereby identified as the author
of this work in accordance with section 77 of the
Copyright, Designs and Patents Act 1988.

A CIP Catalogue record for this book is available from
the British Library.

The publisher acknowledges the financial support of
the Books Council of Wales. www.gwales.com.

Printed and bound in Great Britain by Clays Ltd,
Elcograf S.p.A.

ISBN 9781802584141

1 2 3 4 5 6 7 8 9

THE
JOURNEY

MAGGIE OGUNBANWO

GRAFFEG

I would like to thank all those who have travelled this journey with me, especially my late Da, who always believed great things of me; my husband and children, who have been with me every step of the way; Christine, the Chukwus and Lizbeth, my friends who made parts of the journey bearable and fun; Nain Jean; my Welsh tutors, Elwyn, Helen, Mark, Browen, who patiently taught through my mischief; my friend Charles, who helped me take my first book from dream to reality, and my publishers, Graffeg, who brought my first and second cookery books to life. Thank you to all who have experienced this journey with me.

Maggie Ogunbanwo

Introduction

Welcome to Maggie's melting pot, from Nigeria to Wales via Essex. Maggie has lived a variety of experiences through food, starting with running Maggie's Exotic Foods, a business providing catering services, mainly focused on African, West Indian and Latino foods. She ran three Sure Start Cafes in Essex, trained nannies, food service providers and young parents in food safety, catering and nutrition, taught money and home management to young families, ran The Melting Pot café in Penygroes, North Wales and authored international Gourmand award-winning cookbook *The Melting Pot* and its plant-based follow-up, *African Twist*. Maggie will be sharing some of these stories, packed with flavour, character and vibrance. The titles of the chapters reflect the highlights or significant moments along the way. Also included are interesting recipes that have been significant as Maggie serves you Naija-style (slang for the country Nigeria).

***

Bread Alone is the title of a novel by Judi Hendricks I read more than seven years ago. It had a romantic storyline, but what I remember most and the reason I kept it on my shelf with my large collection of cookbooks was because of the bread and pastry recipes woven into it. They were described so vividly that I could almost taste and smell the aromas while reading and I was determined to recreate them in my kitchen.

With the knowledge that I was committing a great sin against book lovers,

I turned a fold in each of the pages that had recipes (yes, I dog-eared the pages!) and stored the book among my cookery books for easy retrieval.

Now it is my turn to take you on a part of my journey, from warm, steamy Lagos (my one-year-old first born said of Lagos after her first visit that it reminded her of a room full of whistling kettles), to wet, windy and beautiful North Wales by food. I hope you will have a reason to dog-ear your favourite pages (I promise not to tell anyone) and keep returning to them again and again.

1. The Call

From the age of three until I was twenty-three I lived and went to school in Nigeria, where I discovered my love of and gift for cooking. I recently found a concise business plan that I wrote up on 6th January 1989 with details on how I would own and run a restaurant/snack bar, determined to transform the state of the fast-food industry in Nigeria. Two weeks after I got married, my new husband and I flew to the UK, where we intended to live for ten years before returning.

Seventeen years later and we were still in the UK, based in Essex, and by now, with the birth of my son and daughter, there were four of us.

The whole family and a group of friends went to Pentrefelin on holiday, specifically to Ystumllyn, a rambling home between Criccieth and Porthmadog in Gwynedd, North Wales, an area better known as Snowdonia.

The property was large, with plenty of space for the ten of us to successfully play many rounds of hide and seek. Part of the welcome there contained the history of the property, which told us that it used to be the home of John Ystumllyn, also known as Jac Du, or Jack Black, the gardener, who seems to be the first well-recorded black person in North Wales, dating back to the 1800s. Interestingly, as part of the Jubilee celebrations Queen Elizabeth II had a John Ystumllyn rose named for Jac Du and planted in her gardens in May 2022.

As with many of my experiences, I can relate this to a particular dish. In Nigeria, pepper soup is popular as a starter at an event, or, if you are ill and have lost your appetite, it is the go-to cure, a bit like chicken noodle soup in the UK. Just as pepper soup can be served first as a starter, learning about the story of Jac Du was my first introduction to the black history of North Wales, which, unknown to me at the time, I would soon become a part of. Little did I know that this was the start of an enlightening and life-defining holiday for me.

Pepper soup is traditionally made with a mixture of parts of beef, including tripe, kidney pieces, liver, *kpomo* (cleaned cow skin), and can be as hot and spicy as you prefer by the addition of more or less chilli peppers.

Pepper Soup

Serves 4-6
Prep time 25 minutes
Cooking time 40-60 minutes

Ingredients

800g-1kg mixed pieces of beef, cut up into
bite-sized pieces
1.25-1.5 litres water
Pepper soup spices (15ml/1 tablespoon
njangasanga, 2.5ml/½ teaspoon alligator
pepper , 10ml/2 teaspoons black peppercorns,
esekeseke, or a mix of ginger, garlic, paprika,
basil and parsley can be used as a pepper soup
spice alternative)
60ml crayfish or fish sauce
Scotch bonnet/habanero chilli peppers (you can
use a more fiery variety if preferred)
Salt

It is somewhat difficult to suggest all the different
spices that go into making the pepper soup
spice mix, as they differ depending on what
part of Africa or which village you grew up in.
The suggested spices listed above come from
my Cameroonian heritage, but in Nigeria the
spice mix differs. The good thing is that it is now
possible to buy pepper soup spice mixes and just
add as preferred.

Method

1. Place all the spices together with the chillies and crayfish in a food processor or blender and process to a fine puree. You may need to add a little water to move the process along.

2. Place the beef pieces, water, ground spice and chilli mix in a large saucepan and turn the heat setting to high.

3. Bring the contents of the pan to a boil, then turn down the heat and simmer for 40-60 minutes until all the beef pieces are tender.

4. Season to taste with salt and serve hot.

Njangasanga, or njansan, is the African wood oil nut *Ricinodendron africanum, akpi* in Nigeria. *Esekeseke* is the Bakweri name (my mother's language) for *Tetrapleura tetraptera*, also known as 'four corners' because of its shape. In Igbo (the Nigerian language) it is *uhio,* and also commonly found on Google as *prekese.*

I often make my pepper soup plant-based by substituting the meat and crayfish with potatoes, yams or green plantains and thin rice noodles, which are added to a saucepan together with a pre-prepared stock and take less time to cook than beef. Pepper soup can be consumed on its own as a starter or with a side of buns. A recipe for these can be found in my first cookbook, *The Melting Pot*.

On most days during our stay at Ystumllyn, long before anyone got up in the morning, I would go out and explore the area by taking long walks. I was sure I had seen directions to Porthmadog as we were driving around, so on this memorable morning I decided to make my way there. I like to walk with a destination in mind, and though that day's walk was taking a long time, I kept hoping that around every corner I would arrive at Porthmadog.

When I have recounted this story in times past, I have said that I went out for the walk at 5.30am and was out for over two hours, but now I live in the area I realise that this cannot be accurate, as it would have been too dark in April at 5.30am to go out walking in an unfamiliar place. Somewhere on the outbound journey, though, I started to pray, and very quickly my prayers escalated to full-blown, almost uncontrollable crying with huge sobs. I stopped walking and started speaking to God, as I am known to do, asking what was the matter with me and why was I sobbing so deeply. Then I heard a quiet voice saying, 'I want you to pray for my people.'

I literally looked around to ensure I was alone, then I got out my phone and called a trusted friend and ally who at the time was visiting family in Zimbabwe. By now I had settled down enough to talk and recounted to her my recent experience. We talked and prayed around what was happening right there on the road between Criccieth and Porthmadog. I didn't make it to Porthmadog that morning, turning back just before the sign, as I now know, and after what I'd been through I wanted to record the details before I forgot them.

I kept this experience to myself, we had a great holiday and returned home to Harlow in Essex. Two years later, after some soul-searching and disquiet with where we were living, my husband suggested that this would be a good time to move to North Wales.

I protested internally and externally quite strongly, as my life and business seemed to be on an upward trajectory and most of my family and friends were close by, or at least within a thirty-minute drive. In addition, Stansted Airport was handy and except for traffic jams Heathrow and Gatwick were accessible for travel, which we did a fair amount of as a family. The suggestion of moving away from Harlow caused me so much concern that for a while I started losing my hair. I was told it was some form of alopecia (hair loss), brought on by stress in my case.

Then, out of the blue, one day I had a reminder of what I now call 'my epiphany', recalling my experience on the Pentrefelin road and how God had asked me to pray for His people in North Wales. I recalled the discussion with God and my friend in Zimbabwe and finally came to the realisation that it had been preparing me for a change that was to come, one that I would be reluctant to make.

2. The M60 is Leaning to the Right

It was approaching the end of summer 2007, we had sold and moved out of our property in Barn Mead, Harlow, and while waiting to complete all the necessary paperwork for our new property in Penygroes, North Wales, we stayed in temporary accommodation in Longbanks in Harlow for a few months.

This included our family of four: me, my husband Femi and two children aged seven and thirteen, along with our friend Christine, who was moving to Wales with us. This was an intensely busy time as we moved from a four-bedroom house with four people to our three-bed temporary accommodation with five. In that time my mother came to visit and stayed for about three weeks and my husband's sister and husband also visited for about a week. Additionally, the opportunity came for me to travel to Hong Kong and go on to China for the first time with a friend to explore possible trade ideas and I came back with a lot of clothes, bags and jewellery to sell. We had the Longbanks property filled to the brim with what we required for our immediate use and the rest of our stuff was put in storage.

Well, we moved into a dump! Days later we were still trying to live in and clean up the mess left by the previous occupants, scrubbing cupboards, making endless trips to dispose of old carpets and furniture, stripping wallpaper and an endless list of other chores that kept showing up. We needed to leave the property in a good state to be let out on our departure, but we also couldn't live in a dump, so there was a lot of hard work needed to bring the property up to good order.

When I think about that time, it reminds me of how exhausted I felt that I think a break is due for a cup of tea, or *paned,* as we say here in North Wales, and some meat pies. During my upbringing in Nigeria, my mother was a caterer and many of our school lunch boxes contained delightful cupcakes, meat pies and puff-puff, the Nigerian name for a traditional African snack made of fried dough, all reflections of what she and my mother and grandmother produced to contribute to the financial life of our family.

Our friends loved coming round to our house

as there would always be something to eat. In fact, the first thing Marie (the young daughter of our Lebanese neighbour who was convinced our house was her second home) would say in broken English after coming in was, 'You get cake?' My mother would patiently reply for the umpteenth time, 'Say good morning/afternoon, Marie.' So Marie would oblige, 'Good morning, you get cake?' As meat pies are not a staple in Wales but a Nigerian street food, I make my own according to my tried and tested recipe.

Meat Pies
Serves 4-6

Ingredients
Pastry
100g/4oz plain flour
1.75ml/¼ teaspoon salt
1.75ml/¼ teaspoon turmeric
25g/1oz margarine or vegetable oil
100-125ml/¼ pint cold water

Filling
15ml/1 tablespoon vegetable oil
375g/12oz minced beef
1 medium onion, finely chopped
2 cloves garlic, crushed

1 spring onion, finely chopped
5ml/1tsp chili powder or fresh chilli pepper
7.5g/½ tablespoon Maggie's South African curry powder
2.5ml/½ tablespoon dried thyme
2.5ml/½ teaspoon salt or to taste
1.75ml/¼ teaspoon freshly ground black pepper
20g/1oz cracker crumbs, finely ground
50ml/2fl oz stock

For the pastry:

1. Preheat the oven to Gas Mark 7/Fan 220°C assisted 200°C. Place the flour in the bowl of a food processor with the turmeric and salt.

2. Switch the machine to low and add the margarine or vegetable oil. Process for about 30 seconds.

3. Add the water a bit at a time and process until the mixture all comes together in one cohesive ball. You may not need to use up all the water before this happens, or you may require a little more, depending on weather conditions where you prepare this pastry.

4. Turn out the pastry onto a large piece of greaseproof paper or cling film. Cover well and refrigerate till required.

For the filling:
1. In a wok or skillet, heat the oil on a high heat setting for 1-2 minutes.

2. When the oil is hot, add the onions, spring onions and garlic and stir-fry continuously for 2-3 minutes until there is a change in colour.

3. Next, add the minced beef and stir-fry until all the meat is browned, 2-3 minutes.

4. Add the curry spice, chilli, crushed cracker crumbs and thyme and mix in well.

5. Add half of the water/stock and mix in, then bring the contents of the pan to the boil.

6. Turn down the heat and simmer for 20 minutes, stirring from time to time, adding water as required to prevent burning. The mixture should be firm, not sloppy.

7. Taste and adjust the seasonings by adding salt and more chilli pepper if required.

8. Pour off any excess fat or liquid, then set the mixture aside to cool.

For the patties:

1. Bring the pastry out of the fridge and roll out to 5mm thickness.

2. Cut the rolled-out party into rounds using a large pastry cutter or the base of a tortilla press.

3. Place a generous tablespoon (about 60g) of the cooled spiced beef mixture in the middle of the round of pastry.

4. Moisten the edges of the pastry with water using a pastry brush, then fold over and seal using a fork. Alternatively, push the tortilla press together to seal.

5. Repeat until all the mixture is used up. Pierce each meat pie with a fork to create holes for steam to escape during the cooking process.

6. Place the patties on a lightly floured baking tray and bake for about 20-25 minutes or until golden brown.

Enjoy these tasty snacks hot or cold with a drink of your choice, or prepare cocktail-sized meat pies and serve as a starter. I now also make a vegan version using vegetable oil in the pastry and lentil and sweet potatoes or yam and beans for the filling.

The moving date for the journey to North Wales kept being moved forward, as there were complications with what at first seemed a straightforward carrying over of our mortgage from one property to another. What we did not realise at the time was that this was the beginning of the 2007 recession and things had become very precarious in the financial world. In the end our mortgage holders agreed to give us only 30% of our previously agreed mortgage, and this added even more to the stress I was unaware I was under. We had put a full stop to our lives in Harlow and needed to be in Penygroes in time for our children to be able to start a new school year in less than two weeks.

Finally, we were able to negotiate a slightly higher percentage with our mortgage company but had to use the whole of the extra money (equity) that we had made selling our Barn Mead property to make up the balance needed to purchase our new home in Penygroes. While negotiations were progressing, we were also able to make a deal with the owners of the property in Penygroes which involved renting The Red Lion in the village while we waited for the mortgage process to be sorted and the monies to be transferred. As a result, we were finally able to decide on a moving date and time.

The night before moving was a busy and late night making sure the property was left in good order for the new tenants who would be renting it. We would be leaving at midday at the latest for the five-plus-hour drive.

But come midday my husband Femi was still sorting out some last-minute issues that had arisen. When this was done, we started to pack the SUV/people-carrier vehicle we owned at the time ready for the journey but realised that we would not be able to fit everything and everyone in as had been previously planned. The solution was to hire a van. I had mentioned the possibility before the day about the vehicle capacity, but as my husband is such a creative packer and a more laid-back personality than me, he assured me all would be well. I, however, was carrying silent stress about the changes and consequent delay.

Well, all was not well, and we were approaching 4pm. The additional vehicle meant that I would have to drive the people-carrier while my husband drove the van. I had never driven five hours before and I was so tired from the previous night, but I am also a team player, so instead of saying 'I told you so' and mentioning that I was having a recurring ache in the top part of my stomach, I agreed to the change of plan to be driver number two. At that time we weren't using Google or other travel maps on our Nokia phones, so I was going to follow Femi, who had a TomTom navigation system. Again, I did not express that I was not sure I could keep up, as Femi is a much faster and more confident driver than me. I was setting up a cocktail for trouble.

Two hours into the journey, with my trusting seven-year-old son squeezed into the back seat of the vehicle with our belongings and our friend Christine in the front seat beside me, my stomach ache was escalating and the M60 motorway started to lean to the right. To compensate for what I felt, I was veering to the left, causing a big lorry to honk loudly at me and just preventing an accident. My son was asleep, but Christine was aware of what was going on and was praying for me. I decided to join in the prayer and ask God to help me overcome this illusion, and once again I heard that quiet but firm voice say to stop driving.

At this point Femi was a fair way ahead,

Christine had to communicate with him by phone and explain the situation and that it would be necessary for us to stop. We agreed that I should drive as carefully as I could in the slow lane and meet up with the van at the next service station a few miles ahead. I did this with the utmost reluctance and fear and with pain in my stomach, probably crawling along at 35mph in the slow lane and sometimes onto the hard shoulder, but I made it.

At the service station we decided that all I needed was a rest and I would feel better in the morning, so we got back into the vehicles and I slowly followed the lead van. I don't think that Femi has ever driven that slow on a motorway, but he had to keep slowing down to ensure that he stayed with my laboured driving.

Next morning, rested and fed, we got back into our respective vehicles, and as soon as I hit the motorway I started to have a major panic attack and immediately drove onto the hard shoulder. The police arrived in no time, and Femi had stopped a bit of a way ahead as well. I explained the situation to them in a trembling voice and they replied that it was dangerous to stop where we were and it was necessary that they get me to move the vehicle. I assured them I did not think I could do this. The solution was they would drive behind me with my husband driving in front in the slow lane up to the next services. With much fear and trepidation, I followed them that far, but I felt like I was breaking down.

It was obvious by this time that I could not make it as the driver to Wales. The solution that was decided and implemented was that my brother-in-law would drive Christine's car with our friend Steven as a passenger to the services, take over the driving from me and Steven would drive Christine's car to North Wales.

It took many months for roads to stop leaning and many years for me not to panic when faced with the need to drive. Having come to live in a small village, however, I had to be able to get around to the shops and to live, so I got back into the vehicle and each time I hit a milestone, like driving to the end of the village or to Caernarfon or Bangor, I would call someone and celebrate. I did all of that driving with clenched, sweaty palms and was always relieved when I finally arrived at my destination.

While I drive so much better and with much more confidence these days, I still have not picked up the courage to make a five-hour journey. A counsellor and therapist told me that I had a panic attack brought on by stress, and this revealed itself even further in my body by me bleeding nonstop for the next three years until I had to have surgical intervention. Eventually the stomach pains also stopped, as it turned out they were also part of my body's response to the stress I was under and was so unaware of that I did not recognise the signs.

3. The Red Lion

According to local legend Jean Hefina Owen (more about her later), The Red Lion used to be a coaching inn and was originally sited across the road from what is now Capel Soar in Penygroes. It was a popular drinking and events destination as she was growing up and she remembers the children being called in afterwards to come and share in the leftover cakes and food. The building was erected on its current site in 1840 and has served as a public house, as The Red Lion Hotel, as a warehouse and in our time as a family dwelling, housing a café, church and food production facility.

Some years into our stay we had the privilege of hosting a sixtieth wedding anniversary for a couple who had held their wedding reception in The Red Lion all those years before. We gave them a tour of the premises as part of their celebration and they told us some history about the building, describing how some of the rooms had been moved about. What was our bedroom used to serve as the main reception and events room, and that explains why it opens directly out onto the garden on the first floor.

We moved from a three-bedroom house in Harlow to the five-bedroom Red Lion and were literally swimming in it initially, but over the years we've managed to fill it. It makes me wonder what we will do with all we have acquired in the last fifteen years when we need to downsize. Six of us moved into The Red Lion in 2007: our family of four, our friend Christine and my late dad. This number has become two, with my dad first having moved out to his own property down the road at Water Street and then passing away. He is now buried in the local cemetery in Penygroes. Christine moved back to Essex and the two children went off to university and are building their own lives elsewhere. So, hubby and I have a choice of rooms in which to sleep in every night or to use to host many friends and at any one time.

My first recollection of visiting The Red Lion after it had been completely vacated by the previous owners was of a very damp building, yellowed with smoke, infused with deep stale damp cigarette smells, and thought that we had made a big mistake.

Three dehumidifiers later, a partially replaced

roof and a lot of living and the property is now much drier and cosier to live in. We have certainly been on a journey of discovery, with one of the first tasks being to pull up all the carpets in the public areas that the smell of cigarette smoke from ages past had seeped into. A wash of the kitchen cupboards revealed that the wood was more pine and less dark wood from nicotine stains. Slowly we could walk out of The Red Lion without smelling of cigarettes and my children tell me we started to smell of food and spices as we took over with our cooking and café.

In the first year at The Red Lion, I ran a series of cooking classes as a way to meet locals, generate an income, and to use up some of the space. These were held in the former main bar room, which had a snooker room below with a full-size snooker table that was left behind by the previous owners. Before we could use this room for classes, we had to clear it out of all the carpentry equipment that had been left behind.

We took the walls back to brick and had them replastered, as well as changing all the windows to the front of the building which had rotted and decayed and added to the dampness that we first encountered. We learnt a lot of new do it yourself skills. Our most exciting project in the old main bar that I remember us carrying out involved taking down the old ceiling. It was at this time that I first heard of the term lath and plaster. Lath and plaster ceilings and walls were common in houses built from the 1700s right up until the early 1900s and were certainly evident in The Red Lion. Laths are thin strips of wood, around 25mm wide, covered in a lime-based plaster that has often been combined with coarse animal hair, such as goat or horse, for added stability and flexibility.

The laths are nailed horizontally directly to the ceiling joists before the lime plaster mix is worked into the gaps between the laths. Once this has dried out, further coats of plaster are applied before a paint finish. It is said that it is best to leave them alone but ours needed to be gutted and replaced with modern gypsum and plasterboard as well as fitting insulation at the same time. All this was in preparation for using the room as a food/café place.

Every day our team of helpers, family and recruited volunteers, including a friend called Liz who we inherited for a short while, would cover our hair, put on builders' masks and goggles and get to work. All this protective gear was needed to prevent us from inhaling the limestone dust or having bits enter our eyes. Some of us had the task of hacking away at the ceiling above, while others stayed at ground level and cleared the floor. I cannot remember the number of skips we filled and was grateful that we met someone in the early days who could provide us a skip service at a much-reduced rate. At the end of a satisfying day's work, we would all end up covered in white dust from the plaster and need to wash thoroughly before preparing and sitting down to lunch or dinner. In this way, by doing the groundwork we were able to make the small amount of income we had coming in between us all stretch, so that we could afford to pay for the main building work to be carried out by professional builders.

Another interesting development in those days was the garden. It had a form of order but had overgrown and we were unable to maintain it ourselves alongside trying to settle in and make a living. I set out to find a gardener and after a few enquiries and searching the Yellow Pages, the telephone directory, which was still quite popular and used more than Google then for such searches, I found one. I was oh so naïve as I look back on this time. We agreed on a price based on the location of the garden being on the first and not the ground floor. I thought the price quoted was a bit much based on our tight budget, but it needed to be done. What I failed to do at the time was agree the number of hours of work that would be done; I just wanted the space cleared and usable. After about five hours of work on day one and another five on day two, with a lot of work still needing to be done, I realised that this job could spread into many hours. When I enquired how much longer it would take to get the garden to maintenance stage, I was informed that because of its state it would be difficult to predict, it could apparently extend into endless hours. Eventually, I had to learn gardening skills along with some negotiation skills as we could not afford to pay a gardener long term and put an end date on the engagement of the hired gardener.

On one of our holidays while living in The Red Lion we vacationed in Morocco, and we had these delightfully coloured spongy pancakes known as *baghrir* for breakfast. I was so impressed by them that I asked to be shown how to make them by our housekeeper. Not only did she do this, but as a parting gift she gave me a local ceramic bowl that is traditionally used in preparing the dough for semolina galettes that she also served us, along with the vibrant coloured powders that were used to give the Moroccan pancakes their eye-catching, mouth-watering colours.

The ceramic dough bowl was too heavy

and awkward to put in our suitcase, so Femi fashioned a rope basket and I brought it back to The Red Lion as my hand luggage and used it several times to make the pancakes. But do not fear, it is possible to make the pancakes without my Moroccan kneading bowl. I have given them my own twist and serve them for dessert for the customers delight with a mango sauce or syrup or even ice cream.

Ingredients
Serves 6-12
Prep time 10 minutes
Cooking time 25 minutes

300g semolina, fine
150g plain flour
5ml/1 teaspoon salt
7g/1 sachet baking powder
460ml warm water
10ml/2 teaspoons instant yeast
5ml/1 teaspoon caster sugar
2 mangoes, ripe
Water, as required

Method

1. Place the semolina, plain flour, salt and baking powder into a large bowl and stir well until mixed in.

2. Add warm water, instant yeast and sugar to the semolina and flour mixture and mix in well until you have a smooth, creamy mixture.

3. To colour the pancakes, divide the creamy mixture into three bowls. Add a drop or two of green colouring to one bowl and red colouring to another, leaving the last bowl for a cream-coloured pancake.

4. Set aside for a few minutes until several bubbles form on the top.

5. Lightly grease a small pancake pan with a bit of oil and place on medium heat.

6. When hot, place a ladle of pancake mixture in the pancake pan and cook on one side only for about three minutes until several bubbles form and the pancake is cooked. Adjust the heat to make sure the bottom of the pancake browns without burning by the time the top is cooked. Do not turn.

7. Remove the pancake from the pan and set aside, covered, to keep warm. Repeat the process with the rest of the pancake mixture until it is all used up.

8. Serve hot with a mango sauce, jam or even ice cream.

9. Wash the mangoes under running water.

10. With a sharp vegetable knife, peel off all the green skin.

12. Separate all the yellow flesh from the stone using the vegetable knife and chop the flesh into small pieces. Place them in a large bowl.

13. Add a little water to the mango pieces, then, using a hand blender, whizz them to a smooth paste.

14. Stir in 2-3 teaspoons of sugar.

15. Place the mango and sugar mix in a small pan with a bit more water and heat through until the sauce turns shiny.

16. Serve drizzled over the pancakes or in a side bowl.

Two years after moving into The Red Lion in Penygroes, we opened a church in the newly refurbished main bar, and two years after that we opened The Melting Pot café/Y Grochan Flasus in the same space. We added pop- up restaurants, tried to hire out the smaller bar for meetings and functions and in 2016 began producing African-inspired sauces and spice mixes from what had previously been the café kitchen. Part of our refurbishment had included installing a small but professional kitchen whose building was supported by a grant from the local council.

Living and working at The Red Lion has been a huge growth experience for me with many firsts, including my first grant, my first time engaging with a council's planning division (now there is another story), my first experience of farmers and local produce markets as a producer, first café, pop-up restaurant, first taste of deer, venison, wild boar crocodile, first time wallpapering a whole room (I found I was quite good at it). It has been a place of great inspiration and muscle building, both in a literal sense and building the muscles of my mind and heart.

4. Must We Go to School?

The Red Lion was delightful but still terribly damp and we did our best to try and settle in quickly, as the school term was due to start three days after our arrival.

We visited the local schools, Ysgol Dyffryn Nantlle and Ysgol Bro Lleu, senior and junior schools respectively, to get to know what the requirements were and buy uniforms before the opening day.

They are lovely surroundings, with the junior school occupying quaint old buildings and the senior school painted in a green colour that made you wonder if someone had donated free paint. At the time of writing this the paint on the senior school has been changed to a neutral beige.

Both schools are within walking distance from The Red Lion and opposite each other, so on the first day we walked to school with the young ones. We found an all-white, Welsh-speaking population in both schools whose lessons were all held through the medium of Welsh and handouts were given to those who were English speaking in the senior school. Our expectations had been different based on previous information from the school about their bilingual nature.

After the first day, both my children decided that they didn't want to go back to a school where there were no familiar faces and cried every morning for that first week. It was heartbreaking for me. I asked myself more than once if I should let them off, and felt like a bad mum when I insisted they go to school. My reasoning was that if they missed just one day they would be unable to go back and so the quicker they got used to it the better. I am grateful that I had compliant children, as I realise now that they could have dug their heels in and created chaos. They were going through their own emotional rollercoaster of being thrown in at the deep end of a new environment and new language in a village where most of the school population had never seen nor interacted with a black person face to face.

In those early days, while getting to know the local community and the communities in the local churches we hosted a lot of visitors on a very tight budget. All financial reserves had gone into paying our mortgage deficit, I had given up my cafes, so Femi was travelling back and forth to Harlow for work and was the main wage-earner for us all. So we served all visitors the first thing they would be likely to be served if they visited Nigeria for the first time: Jollof rice which wasn't too expensive to prepare ingredients.

In *The Melting Pot*, my first cookbook, we provided a simple chicken jollof recipe, so here I share with you another modified rice dish. A simple, tasty and colourful savoury rice with a Maggie twist, this was served to many visitors to The Red Lion in those early days. Though based on using pre-cooked basmati rice, you can use any leftover rice.

To cook basmati rice, you need 60g to 100g per person, depending on if this is to serve as a side or main dish. You need exactly one and a half times the amount of water to get perfectly cooked basmati rice each time, so I advise that you weigh out the water. If I was organised enough, I would cook my rice early and then run it through several changes of cold tap water to cool it completely, drain, place in a bowl and cover. The cooked drained rice can then be set aside in the fridge or a cool place until needed to prepare the recipe.

Maggie's Quick Savoury Rice
Serves 4-6

Ingredients
360g basmati rice
500g water
2.5ml/½ teaspoon ground cumin
2.5ml/½ teaspoon ground coriander
1.5ml/pinch or two turmeric
2.5ml/½ teaspoon salt, or according to taste
2.5ml/½ teaspoon chilli powder (optional)
2.5ml/½ teaspoon paprika (optional)
5ml/1 teaspoon vegetable oil or butter

Method
1. Wash the basmati rice in several changes of cold water until the water runs clear and is no longer cloudy. Drain through a sieve or colander.

2. In a medium saucepan, add the rice, water and salt and place over high heat. Bring the contents of the pan to the boil, then turn down the heat to low, place a tight-fitting lid on the saucepan and simmer for 10 to 12 minutes until all the water runs dry. Best to time this.

3. At this point you can cool the rice down and stop the cooking process by running it under cold water until the rice is completely cool. This will prevent the rice from sticking.

4. To prepare the savoury rice, add the 5ml/1 teaspoon of oil or butter to a wok or non-stick frying pan and place over medium heat.

5. Add the cumin, coriander and turmeric to the oil and mix in. Add the rice to the oil, cumin, coriander and turmeric mix and stir-fry over high heat, mixing in thoroughly until all the rice grains are coated with the spice mix. Add a drop or two of water if necessary to prevent the rice from burning.

6. Keep stir-frying until the rice is heated through, 5 or more minutes depending on the pan you are using. Serve it hot with a side of cooked peas, as the colours combine nicely on a plate, and a Naija stew or curry.

If you want to serve up a hot spicy rice, then use the 5ml of chilli powder. If you wanted to serve up a golden rather than a yellow-colored savoury rice, then the paprika should be used as when combined with the turmeric produces a lovely golden orange rice dish.

Any cooked left-over rice can be used as a basis for a lovely colourful rice salad.

In this recipe slightly less water has been used for boiling the rice, because we don't want the savoury rice to become sticky when we stir-fry it.

My children continued going to their school for a week, but then they had another change: they had to go to Welsh language immersion school for the next term so they could better fit into their local schools eventually. In a way this was a bit of a reprieve for us all as Welsh language immersion classes were populated with others like them who were new to the environment and the language and the classes were smaller, so they did not feel as out of place as they had felt in their other *ysgolion* (schools).

I remember the head of the junior immersion school telling the new parents that in the first week they taught the new students 100 Welsh words using the medium of English and after that they communicated only in Welsh, using and building on those 100 words for the rest of the student's time there. I would have loved to have been a part of that Welsh learning experience.

They settled in and learnt the Welsh language

while I immersed myself after week two in part-time Welsh language classes. They returned to their respective junior and senior schools promising that once they graduated and left Penygroes they would never return to Wales.

After graduating, my daughter worked for a year as a physiotherapist in Ysbyty Gwynedd, the local hospital, and my son is currently doing the circuit round North and South Wales rapping/drilling through the Welsh language. They survived and are doing well, and I get by in Welsh!

5. The Airport Café

As Africans and particularly of Nigerian origin, we can hardly be found eating just a rice dish on its own. This would usually be accompanied by a sauce or curry and a protein. So, while I will share with you the continuing journey of my settlement into the small Welsh village called Penygroes, I will also share my spiced meatballs in a chunky tomato sauce recipe.

In some ways the tomato sauce ingredients remind me of the 'stew' you would experience at mealtime if you stayed in a Nigerian home for any period of time. I have modified this recipe in many ways over the years and it reflects some Italian influence, as I did a short stint as a chef in an Italian restaurant in the past and taught classes on Italian cookery.

Tomatoes are plentiful in summer and if, like me, you are a budding gardener on and off, you may have a few of your own. The thing is I always end up with more green than ripe ones (these make a fantastic pickle, but that is a recipe for another book).

Ripe, luscious red tomatoes made into a spicy tomato sauce can be cooked in bulk and frozen in small batches to take out of the freezer and used when a time-saving meal is required. We have loads of cheap tomatoes during the summer season in Nigeria, but unfortunately we are never guaranteed a constant supply of electricity and so cannot constantly run a freezer. With the rise of technological innovation, it is becoming possible to run individual electric items powered by solar energy and this will make it possible to preserve our sauces and a whole load of other produce by freezing long term. You can make your sauce as hot and spicy as you wish by increasing or decreasing the chilli sauce levels. The cumin and cinnamon in the meatballs suggest a hint of North Africa.

Plain Tomato Sauce
Serves 4-6
Prep time 20 minutes
Cooking time 45-50 minutes

Ingredients
500g/1lb tomatoes, skinned, or 1 x 395g can plum tomatoes
1 small onion
1 stick celery

1 clove garlic
1 bay leaf
1 sprig parsley
5ml/1 teaspoon sugar
Salt and freshly ground black pepper, to taste

Method
1. Place all the ingredients into a saucepan and bring to the boil, then simmer uncovered for 30 minutes.

2. Discard the bay leaf, then use the sauce as it is, or, for a smoother sauce, rub through a fine sieve or blend in a food processor and set aside.

Meatballs
Ingredients
1 slice thick bread
450g lean minced beef/lamb or poultry
5ml/½ teaspoon ground cinnamon
5ml/½ teaspoon ground cumin
5ml/1 teaspoon Maggie's original chilli sauce
Salt and black pepper, to taste

Method
1. Soak the bread for a few minutes in water, then squeeze and drain well.

2. Place the bread and mince into a mixing bowl and beat vigorously with a wooden spoon until the mixture is pasty. This can also be done by hand.

3. Add the cinnamon, cumin, salt, chilli sauce and black pepper and mix in well.

4. With floured hands, shape the meat mixture into about 16 meatballs and place on a baking tray, evenly spaced out.

5. Place the tray of meatballs in a preheated oven at 180°C/Gas Mark 6 for 12-15 minutes.

6. Add the meatballs to the chunky or smooth tomato sauce and bring back to a simmering boil over medium heat. Heat through and serve on a bed of golden yellow savoury rice.

You can also serve the meatballs on their own on a bed of green salad with a cocktail stick placed into each one as part of a canape buffet. I would make 32 meatballs to serve as canapes.

***

As non-Welsh speakers, finding jobs was a difficult process for us. Femi applied for over a hundred jobs and got one interview, Christine got a job as a housekeeper with Trigonos, a retreat centre in a neighbouring village, where the team were English, and I eventually got a job as a part-time cook in Caernarfon Airport café, which was run by English Roy and his team. A whole load of jobs required a knowledge of the
Welsh language none of us had at the time, but the Caernarfon Airport team were happy for me to continue Welsh lessons twice a week if there was someone to cover the kitchen, and this was a key requirement for me.

The job was convenient as it was less than five miles from The Red Lion and driving was still a struggle for me. It also meant that I was able to be back before the end of the school day.

Caernarfon Airport café was housed in an interesting building. At the top was the airport's watchtower, reached via a set of rusted, characterful iron stairs. I had never been into an airport tower before, so this was a lovely addition to the café for me. Below the café seating area was a good-sized kitchen and the offices. The café had so many holes in the walls that you could hear wind whistling through all day and sometimes you could feel the kitchen sway if there was a heavy storm and I would feel tempted to hold onto a beam.

I settled down to my new job by giving a thorough and well-needed spring clean to the kitchen and café areas while wondering how they had survived the environmental health visits up to that time. Despite its dilapidated state, it was a nice, friendly environment to work in, the staff and visiting pilots were a delight to get to know and they appreciated a bit of spicing up of the menu.

The other part-time chef, who was more experienced than I in hotel kitchen work, did not last very long, so in the end the café became my baby and I was allowed a free hand. Every day they wondered what new item I would put up on the menu and how it would taste this time, as up until then I had not started using any standard recipes that I could repeat time and again – I cooked from instinct each time. For six months I worked in that café like it was my own, engaging any member of my family who happened to visit us in Wales to come and work with me for free.

This was an opportunity that began to open up to me the food and drink world in Wales, from Harlech food service and Brake Bros food distribution company to Posh Puds, the cheesecake specialists based on Anglesey, as well as farmers' markets and local producers. I met local Welsh celebrity chefs like Mel Thomas and even did a few recordings with Dudley Newbury for TV while speaking in Welsh. They tell me I did well, but I cannot remember what I said and can't be sure I didn't just make it all up.

I worked happily at the airport café for six months, and in that time a new development started there to incorporate new, larger aeroplane hangars, new offices, a state-of-the-art café/kitchen space and even a flight simulator. I was involved in helping to set up the new kitchen ready for its opening, and in the meantime another part-time cook joined the team.

We were really looking forward to the opening day of the new facility and planned it to be grand and showcase the kind of menu our brand-new site was going to offer, but unfortunately the airport team and I had to part ways and the other cook had the pleasure of finishing what I started.

While I had not expected my departure to be so quick, it turned out to be timely, as it gave me the opportunity to set up my own little café space at The Red Lion in what would have formerly been the bar area, a space that several in the community remember visiting for occasions and celebrations with their families back in the fifties and sixties. You can still find a café at Caernarfon airport, which now houses the Air Ambulance Service.

6. The Melting Pot Café/ Y Crochan Flasus

My father, who had lived in the next estate to us in Harlow, eventually decided to move to Penygroes so he could once again be near our family. Born in Zaria, Nigeria, with a substantial property in Lagos, he chose to relocate himself to a small village in an 80 percent Welsh-speaking village so as not to be isolated and alone. He filled up most of his time going back and forth to Ysbyty Gwynedd for various types of hospital appointments that assured his continuous health and by walking up the hill from his house to ours.

He had recently been on a trip to Spain with my oldest brother, who lived in Denver, USA. He flew into Manchester and came to Penygroes solely for the purpose of taking a road trip by air with Daddy. While in Spain a health situation arose that saw my father taken by ambulance to a local hospital where, to rectify an obstruction, the hospital had to fit a temporary catheter.

A few days after arriving back in Wales he was in agony, so I called an ambulance. Before we got into the ambulance, he insisted on writing two cheques. One was for completing the work that would enable me to open my new café and the other was for his first grandson to be able to get into a local college in Bangor to study fashion design. I was baffled at his insistence, but he was determined that this should be done.

At the hospital they found out that my father had an infection brought on by the insertion of the catheter, which they would have to take out in a minor procedure, but he never returned home from that hospital visit and died from septicaemia after his operation.

That was in March of 2010 and in November of the same year I opened The Melting Pot café, also known as Y Grochan Flasus. The naming of the café caused loads of debate but I was encouraged to have a Welsh name for my café, for obvious reasons.

This was the fulfilment of a long-held dream which I had first documented in detail in 1998 (this was in another one of my plans I found some years back) and my late father, who had been a great champion of mine, had facilitated this as one of his last actions in this world. My hero!

The journey from zero to opening day is longer than this chapter will allow, but in summary, it involved many volunteers, pulling down lath and plaster ceilings, engaging the local planning division of the council (several times and with many tears), learning a lot of new things, negotiating for services on a limited budget, engaging my first-ever grant process through Gwynedd council's local investment fund, finding accountants and suppliers. In truth as I look back on the exhausting list of firsts at a time when I had just lost my father, I feel overwhelmed all over again and so this is a good time to take a breather from my recollections and talk about *foofoo*.

Foofoo, foufou, fufu, sadza, nsima (nshima), ugali – there are several different forms of this dumpling-type dough that are served as a staple all over Africa, usually accompanied by a stew filled with vegetables and usually some kind of protein.

The name may indicate what a particular *foofoo* is made from: *sadza*, popular in Zimbabwe, is made from maize/corn flour, *eba*, popular in Nigeria, is made from fermented cassava, *amala* is made from yam flour and *tuwo shinkafa*, popular in northern Nigeria, is made from rice. I just realised that I could write a whole book just on *foofoo* as there are so many different permutations, including the more contemporary ones that have become popular as they are considered to be lighter and more supportive of a healthier lifestyle, such as oatmeal *foofoo* and potato and cornflour *foofoo*.

This is a fairly simple staple to prepare, the complexities come depending on which grain flour you are using and how much water is needed. *Fufu* is cooked over medium heat and stirred with sufficient water until a thick, dough-like consistency is achieved. The resulting *fufu* is then shaped into a variety of different and pleasing-to-the-eye shapes and served with *efo riro* (which also features in my cookbook *The Melting Pot*), or some other native stew.

In Penygroes, with Nain Jean and my adult learning Welsh language classes we had such discussions and conversations around the correct translation of The Melting Pot: which was grammatically correct, Y Crochan Blasus or Y Grochan Flasus? In my classes I was taught the correct grammatical way, but my Penygroes locals were not having it. Which way to go? I was living and serving the people of Penygroes, so we settled on Y Grochan Flasus.

We opened our café doors in November 2010 with great menu ideas, including the plan to serve full breakfast until 11.30am and not serving chips, instead opting for a healthier menu, and very quickly had to revise this. I watched potential customers walk out as we weren't serving breakfast when they came in at lunchtime, and no chips either, so we adjusted to what customers were asking for. We were also asked why there wasn't any Nigerian or spicy food on the basic menu, so once again we modified this to offer options like our spicy Nigerian omelette and pepper soup.

If you were a more adventurous traveller to Wales or if you came to one of The Melting Pot cafe's African evenings, you would have been served with or experienced the delight of *fufu*. These versatile dumplings come in different shapes and sizes made from many types of grains or root vegetables and served with native soups. Let me share with you the recipe for *eba* made with cassava granules, as it was the most common *foofoo* I ate while growing up in Nigeria and still eat here in Wales.

Just when we thought it would be straightforward, I must mention that there are different types of cassava granules and they absorb water differently. The *eba* I remember eating most as a child in Nigeria was prepared with white cassava granules, to which one just added boiling water. I could never get it right by directly adding boiling water to the cassava granules in a bowl, it turned out either too hard or soft or not enough water, so I find the version cooked on the cooker top the most precise. It is possible to prepare *eba* in the microwave also, so have fun experimenting.

Less often, more commonly when we visited Cameroon, we had yellow *eba*, but at that time I preferred the less tangy, more subtle flavour of yellow *garri* to that of Ijebu *garri*. As I have grown older, I have come to appreciate strong, tangy Ijebu *garri*, perhaps because my husband is Ijebu culturally.

A mention of *garri* will not be complete without talking about the way it was most enjoyed in secondary school, then and now, as a type of uncooked custard, or drinking *garri,* as it is called, with ice cold water and sugar. Variations including the addition of milk, peanuts and even honey. As a toddler, my son revealed his Ijebu heritage by choosing drinking *garri* as one of his favourite foods.

Eba/Foofoo
Serves 2-4
Prep time 5 minutes
Cooking time 6-8 minutes

Ingredients
White *garri* granules (You need about 1/3 to 1/2 cup of garri granules to 1 cup of boiling water)
Boiling water

Method
1. In a kettle, boil just enough water for your eba.

2. Measure out one cup of boiling water and add to a medium-sized saucepan.

3. Place the saucepan over medium heat, and stir in the *garri* granules, using a wooden or plastic spatula.

4. Keep stirring until the required soft or harder consistency is achieved and the dough forms a cohesive ball that pulls away from the sides of the pan.

5. We are now ready to roll into shapes and serve, so turn off the heat but leave the pan in place while shaping.

Shaping can be a process or art form all of itself. The simplest way I learned was to take a portion of the eba using the spatula, place it into half a calabash and roll it around to a smooth ball.

You had to first wet the inside of the calabash with a little bit of water to prevent the eba from sticking to the sides.

The calabash, also known as *igba* in Yoruba or *duma* in Hausa, is an interesting piece of equipment in the Nigerian kitchen which can also have designs carved or burnt into it and serve as a household decoration or be turned into a musical instrument. Calabashes are made from mature gourds which have been hollowed out and dried.

On the matter of shaping, in the absence of a half calabash it is simple enough to spoon out a portion-sized dollop with a spatula, then, using another spoon, ease this gently onto a plate and smooth it out to a pleasing shape.

Alternatively, and perhaps a little more non-traditional and fancier, lay down a wide piece of cling film or beeswax wrap and place a dollop of *eba* in the middle, lay another piece of cling film/beeswax wrap over the *eba* dollop and press down with the flat of your palm. Using a rolling pin, roll the *eba* flat, remove the top cling film and use a table knife to gently but neatly cut the edges to a rectangle or square shape. Using the bottom clingfilm, gently push the *eba* square or rectangle into a roll and serve with your chosen stew.

The Melting Pot café opened with a flourish, with the help of family and friends. We then had to face the business of employing staff, increasing our real customer base and keeping the menu interesting and varied. We met many characters, had many laughs, experienced a few unfavourable customer reviews and continued to think up novel ways to bring in customers. We held special evenings, decorated the café and created a menu which we advertised beforehand in the window and on our growing Facebook page. It was my personal page, as I knew next to nothing about how to use social media platforms and business pages. A memorable evening was our USA barbeque event, where we featured burgers with an African twist, antelope, deer, wild boar to mention a few and loads of fries.

Y Grochan Flasus served the local community for just over four years, and in the end was known for its Mega breakfast that was served all through the day from 8.30am to 3pm, Monday to Saturday. It had its regulars, most well-known and popular of all was of course Jean Hefina Owen, who lived just down the road. She was known to say that the café saved her life and was very disappointed when I chose to close it down.

After that time she attended every single one of the African evenings we ran until lockdown put a stop to them and Miss Jean took her exit from Penygroes and the world permanently at the grand age of eighty-one. Miss Jean became a part of our café during that time, visiting in the morning and just before closing time, and spoke to everyone like she was the Mayor of Penygroes.

From these evenings the purpose of The Melting Pot café morphed from being a source of income for us to an opportunity to bring Africa to North Wales. I became aware as time went by that some of the residents of my village would never cross the bridge to visit neighbouring Anglesey, never mind visiting Africa. We were therefore going to bring Africa to them via food, and from there the idea of running African evenings in Penygroes was born.

I did not have a plan to shut down the café within four years, but as the journey of life holds unknown twists and turns, I was unable to function properly health wise. That meant I had to reduce my load, making closing the café painful but necessary, and the final decision took me a while to execute as I was aware that the livelihoods of my staff would be affected.

7. African Evenings in Penygroes

While the café was running, we started our series of special event evenings to introduce foods from other countries to the local and wider community in what we called pop-up restaurants (in some circles they are called supper clubs).

I would research a particular type of food or country, including its main and national dishes, its famous landmarks and people, decorating the space and converting it into a restaurant-type setting to reflect the chosen country and food of the month.

I would then prepare a three or more-course menu and share it with customers in the café, at food markets and via email. We began with our successful American burger evening, where we served wild boar and apple, deer and zebra burgers and sausages among others American style, and had the support of my family and some enthusiastic ideas, especially from my daughter.

Following on from these we began a tour

around the continent of Africa through the medium of food. We decorated the wall with a map of Africa and a pin highlighting the country we were showcasing. We bought and put up the relevant flag and decorations that we either got from our collection or which were loaned to us by Dr Simon, our regular customer who had travelled extensively across the African continent. We developed quizzes relating to the country based on the information around the room and offered prizes to the winning groups or tables. They were fun evenings that required a lot of preplanning and so I depended on the good will of family and any friends I could recruit, paid and unpaid. Christine, my friend, was very good at doing the research and writing up the menus once I developed them – the evenings would have been impossible without her support. My family would offer their help as often as they were able, and that day's dinner would be whatever was left over from the evening's menu.

Our African evenings ran for just over three years and visitor numbers varied, with our Moroccan evening being the most successful one that I remember. We had two sittings with about sixty people in total and because I had recently been on a trip to Morocco, I made delicious and colourful Moroccan pancakes and invited a belly dancer. The belly dancer had to manoeuvre and dance around our tightly fitted space in shimmery belly-revealing wear, which was a hit with some but not all of our guests.

We started getting invitations to hold pop-up restaurants in different locations so what started as African evening in Penygroes popped up in Camaes Bay, Pentrefelin, Llanfairfechan and several other venues around North Wales. We featured Hawaiian, Cuban, Cameroonian and Nigerian menus and in total visited over forty African countries by food, sometimes more than once, before the lockdowns caused by Covid-19 put a stop to indoor functions.

Here is a sample of the information we would place on the tables while the café was open which would be written up in English and Welsh. This was written up in English and Welsh:

Hello and welcome to The Melting Pot.

I am Maggie and I would like to introduce you to Africa, where I come from originally.

There are 43 countries that make up the horn of the African continent.

I grew up in Nigeria, so we will start there.

Please feel free to look at the wall showing pictures, fabrics, and some info about the country.

Please ask about our Nigerian food on the menu and our spice of the month, have a taste and do come back next month to follow our journey to the next country.

Nigeria: Small coast, landlocked to the west, north and east
Motto: Unity, Faith, Peace & Progress
Population: 167 million (2011)
Languages: Hausa, Igbo, Yoruba
Currency: Naira (1 GBP = 250 Naira)
Food Type: Uses many different spices, herbs and flavourings with palm oil or groundnut oil to create deeply flavoured sauces and soups, often made very hot with chilli peppers.
(At the present time the conversion rate for the Nigerian currency is 1GBP = 750 Naira.)

We had visitors from Penygroes and the surrounding towns and villages as well as from Anglesey and Manchester, but our most popular visitors were Nain Jean and Dr Simon and his two boys. The youngest would have been about five years old when they first attended and was a very enthusiastic eater. He tried everything, and sometimes more than once.

Nain Jean attended every single one of our evenings and always asked for a cup of tea, whether it was on the menu or not. She would pay for a child's portion and then avoid anything she didn't recognise at first. As time went by, she would give everything on the menu a try at least once, if she was assured it wouldn't 'burn her mouth'. On our last evening before the pandemic resulted in the lockdowns, Nain Jean, who was almost eighty years old at the time, got up on a table and danced to the live music that we provided. This amused some of the guests and created great concern for others, so I had to be called in from the kitchen to persuade her to come down. In truth this reflected how friendly and relaxed our evenings had become over the years, with Nain Jean chatting to every guest at every table like she was holding court while I controlled the quality and flow of food coming out of the kitchen.

Dr Simon and his boys would ask for a menu afterwards and created an album of all the African Evening menus, including the ones they were unable to attend. They also followed the pop-up around and visited us in Pentrefelin, Llanfairfechan and other locations.

I discovered a lot about the food of Africa while taking this journey and about the clear differences in the north, south, east and west of the continent around their use of chillies in their cooking.

West Africa is known for its hot stews and

soups, and some south African countries which have been influenced by Indian cooking use a lot of piri piri chillies in their dishes, while in east and north Africa the use of chillies in cooking is greatly reduced.

Whenever we featured a West African country on the menu, instead of making a dish unbearably hot for all our customers, I started creating different hot sauces to go with the different countries' menu. It was through this process of creating a side hot chilli dish for one of our evenings that the sauces that now make up a popular part of the product range of Maggie's African Twist were born.

My first reaction to this sauce was, 'Wow!' This was confirmed by so many others who tried it that evening, including family. I was encouraged to bottle and sell the sauce by many voices and here began my journey into the unknown but which was the fulfilment of a younger Maggie's dreams.

Sample Nigerian Menu in 2013:

STARTERS

Nigerian Noodle Pepper Soup: a hot, light, and spicy soup with African herbs and spices V 3.50

Pumpkin and Ginger Soup: seasonal creamy soup with lots of fresh ginger £3.20

Cocktail Chicken with Limunga's sauce: chicken bites marinated in parsley, chives, and basil, coated in breadcrumbs and lightly fried £3.95

Black Eye Bean and Spinach Brochettes: Light and puffy balls on a layer of ciabatta and spinach V £3.25

Prawns in Batter with Garlic and Lemon Mayo: Giant prawns in a light and crispy batter £4.25

MAINS

Aunty Francesca's Spicy Oxtail Stew: Succulent oxtail on the bone in a rich spicy curry like stew with African and West Indian flavours £8.95

Chicken Jollof Rice with Fried Plantains (Dodo): Nigerian celebration dish with a tasty, tantalising mix of herbs, spices, and tomatoes £7.95

Naija Goat Meat Stew: Pieces of goat meat on the bone marinated and cooked in a mouth-wateringly tasty red curry like stew £9.95

Black eyed bean curry (Ewa) with fried Plantain and Bewole: Rich bean casserole, sweet dodo and stir fry

of greens V £5.95
Egusi Pudding /melon seed loaf: Jewelled melon seed loaf with succulent bits of beef and dried fish £9.95

All Mains Served with Naija Fried Rice or Potatoes and seasonal vegetables
(No extra rice or potatoes with Jollof rice meal)

DESSERTS

Bread and Butter Pudding with Cream or Ice Cream: Homemade, rich dessert £2.50
Maggie's Heavenly Cheesecake: with mango and passion fruit £3.25
Homemade Apple Crumble with Custard: with our delicious crumbly topping £2.75
Selection from display

Apart from different types of hot sauces, one common side dish in our pop-up restaurants would be plantains, which the customers would get to try in many forms. Plantains are like big bananas but are in fact a vegetable that must be cooked in a similar way to how you would cook potatoes. If we were being truly scientific then plantains are described as a fruit, but they have tougher outer skins than bananas that must be peeled with a knife. They can be eaten at all stages of their ripeness, from the green unripe plantains that I used to eat growing up, a Cameroonian staple, to the yellow, ripe but firm. In colder weather, as they ripen, plantains become black on the outside and very sweet on the inside and can be made into a fritter or a cake.

The most popular way of cooking and serving yellow ripe plantains is sliced and fried, known as *dodo* (*dohdoh*) in this form in Nigeria.

Fried plantains are quite common around the continent as a side, breakfast or main meal, and we show you how to prepare them here.

Fried Plantains/Dodo
Serves 4 as a side dish
Prep time 5 minutes
Cooking time 6-8 minutes

Ingredients
2 yellow plantains (yellow to black are better than green to yellow)
300-400ml vegetable oil, for frying
Salt (optional)

Method
1. Using a sharp vegetable knife, cut off the top and tail of the plantain.

2. Cut a slit lengthways from top to bottom in the skin of the plantain. Using your fingers, ease the skin away from the inner flesh of the plantain to reveal a creamy coloured, banana-looking flesh. Discard the outer flesh.

3. Lay the peeled plantain on a chopping board and cut into even 2cm rounds and set aside. You can add salt at this point.

4. Meanwhile, place a large, heavy-based frying pan over low heat on the cooker top and add all the vegetable oil. Alternatively, you can use a deep fat fryer.

5. When the oil is hot (my mother always used to suggest dropping a small slice of onion into the oil – if it sizzles then the oil is hot enough. This also serves to give the oil a nice flavour). Drop in the plantain slices, ensuring that they are not overlapping.

6. Fry for 2-3 minutes on one side, then, using the tongs, turn the plantain rounds over until they are golden brown on each side.

These can be served hot as a starter, as a side to a rice dish, for breakfast with eggs or, if you are like me, you can just pick at them one at a time when they are cold. Growing up, *dodo* was always salted before frying, but I find that I like plantains without salt and this is one way to reduce salt intake in your diet.

Along with jollof rice, plantains are served often to visitors and are always present as party food at Nigerian events. They have become quite popular in the UK and can be found at ethnic food stores, but also in supermarkets and shops in areas where there is a large migrant community – I order mine through my local greengrocer. Do enjoy.

8. Four Chips and a Slice of Bacon

'My grandmother was a bitch of a woman.' This is how I remember Nain Jean, or Ms. Jean, who was proud to describe herself as Jean Hefina Owen, the Mayoress of Penygroes. She was a character and one of the first people I met when we arrived in the village over fifteen years ago. She made that comment so often and even began writing a book that started with that line, but, sadly, I don't think she completed it.

Nain Jean, meaning Grandma Jean, as we all called her (an old Nigerian custom requires that you do not call anyone over ten years older than you by their first name. While I have largely got round this and adopted the British way, I find it difficult to call people more than twenty plus years older than me by their first name, so I called her what my son called her and those around me followed suit), explained that as a younger person she had thought her own *nain* a very hard woman, and only with time did she realise the burden that she carried, including a tumour the size of a grapefruit that she never sought a doctor about.

That line, however, paints what a character Nain Jean was, attending every single one of our African evenings and leaving on time to catch Simon Cowell on *The X Factor* on TV. She was not happy if there was a delay from the kitchen and did not hesitate to let me know. She was also a regular at The Melting Pot café for a morning *paned* (hot drink) and an afternoon visit and was very unhappy when we had to close down. She often said to me that the café was like a lifeline to her, and she did not know what to do with herself after it closed down.

As a result, Nain Jean and I took to going out every Tuesday at 11am and continued this for more than four years until the lockdowns put a stop to it.

On the occasions that she ordered food in The Melting Pot café she would order a small breakfast or bacon and toast or an egg and toast, as she had a small appetite. When we started café hopping Nain Jean would order a child's portion of soup or whatever she chose from the menu that day, saying that if a large meal was put in front of her she tended to lose her appetite.

As time progressed, she had particular things

she would order at particular cafes, the most popular of which was egg and chips or bacon and chips, but, of course, a child's portion. This progressed to seven chips and a slice of bacon, and she would count the chips and complain and either ask a member of staff if they could remove the excess or she would dump them onto my plate.

In the last year before we had to stop café hopping, she was down to four chips and a slice of bacon, half of which ended up on my plate. Some cafes were unable to accommodate this and so I would order the chips and put four on a plate for Nain Jean. Others had no pricing structure for this strange request, but she was so well known around Penygroes, Caernarfon and Porthmadog that most places we visited just laughed at the quirky Jean and many just charged £1.

Nain Jean always insisted on paying for our meals and we often wrestled to see who could get to the chip and PIN machine first. She reckoned that I was paying for the petrol so she would cover the food. On some occasions Nain Jean and I shared a cake and she told me that was her meal done for the day. I used to wish I could eat like she did.

Jean had the stature of what I call a typical old-school Welsh person that you see in old quarry pictures, small and compact but very strong and determined. She was adamant that she would not eat spicy food at our evenings, but as chips were not often on the menu, I convinced her more than once to try Naija stew and its variations with rice, *eba* and even yam, and she did so after I promised that it did not contain chillies. To be honest, I think Nain Jean's palette changed over the time she spent sharing our company and our food and she spent the last three Christmas days with us eating a child's portion of whatever we prepared.

Learning to cook under my grandmother, who everyone in the neighbourhood fondly called Nana, I learnt to steam chicken Nana-style. This involved cutting up a whole chicken into about fourteen serving pieces. At that time in Nigeria only whole fresh chickens were available, so I also learnt how to buy the best chicken, judging the weight by feel and inspection and shaking each option up and down to determine which would provide the best value for money. It was important to make the decision beforehand by inspecting the chickens visually before asking to handle only two or three (you didn't want to upset the seller by handling too many).

My memories of buying chicken, apart from in the market from a market seller, was outside the home, where you would observe sellers of chicken and various kinds of other produce passing by, calling out proudly in a sing-song voice what goods they had on offer. Chickens were carried in woven baskets on the vendor's head, and once you heard the cry, 'BUY CHICKEN!' (or *adie*, as it is called in the Yoruba language), someone would run out and hail the vendor and the bargaining would begin. You never purchased anything without a bit of bargaining!

Then you would prepare the chicken, pluck its feathers, remove any inedible part and set this aside as part of the dog food that would be prepared later before cutting up the chicken into pieces to be steamed. What is now popularly known in London markets as 'hard chicken' was usually free-range and needed a fair amount of cooking time. Many households reared their own chickens for consumption in their grounds or compounds and you could find through the day many a chicken strutting around like they owned the property. Then came the advent of what was called agric chicken, which were quickly reared chicken for table use and what we commonly have in supermarkets now. Agric chickens are softer, less flavoursome and have a high water content compared to the free-range variety.

So, I learnt to steam tough free-range chickens by placing the fourteen or more pieces in a saucepan with a lid that fit properly. I would add seasonings to the chicken, including chopped onions, salt and chilli pepper, and just enough water to cover the base of the saucepan. I would turn the heat down low, place the lid on the saucepan and let the contents simmer till all the chicken pieces have turned a lighter shade on the outside or till the water runs dry. After this I would add enough water to cover the chicken pieces, bring the contents back to a rolling boil, turn down the heat and simmer on low with the lid on until all the chicken pieces were cooked through. This ensured that all the flavour provided by the onions and spices were absorbed into the chicken pieces. This cooking process could take up to an hour or more depending on the size of the chicken pieces and the amount. The cooked chicken would then be added to Nigerian stew, heated through and served with boiled rice or yams or beans.

With batch-raised chickens that you can buy in the supermarkets or at a local butcher now, the process varies slightly. The chicken is added to the saucepan with the seasonings and onion but no water, covered with a tight-fitting lid and left to simmer for about twenty-five to thirty-five minutes until all the chicken pieces are cooked through and then they are ready to add to the stew.

Nigerian stew, or Naija stew, as it is popularly known, is common in every household and among every tribe in Nigeria, who all have their own way of making it. My Aunty F used to make the best version of the stew which used gravy granules, sage and onion stuffing and many scotch bonnet chillies, mixing in flavours of the UK and Jamaica.

I watched a friend make her version that was heavy on large red peppers and tomato puree boiled up and very little onion, and she added the oil at the end of the cooking process almost like a garnish. It was delicious and she used it as the basis for jollof rice and Efo/Naija vegetable soup, so I have become a collector of Nigerian stew recipes.

I taught a group of four young Italians who were holidaying with me in Penygroes some years ago how to make basic Naija stew and that is the simple-to-recreate recipe I am sharing here. I must mention that each of the four attempts looked and tasted different, even though they had the same recipe, access to the same ingredients and the same kitchen utensils.

Naija Stew

Ingredients
1 small onion (yellow or red)
1 tin peeled plum tomatoes (or crushed tomatoes)
1 red bell pepper
1 clove garlic (peeled)
45-60ml vegetable oil
10ml/2 teaspoons tomato puree
7.5ml-15ml Maggie's Naija This n That spice blend
250-500ml stock
Cooked chicken pieces
5ml Maggie's Original Hot Sauce, or to taste
Salt, to taste

Method
1. Peel the onion, cutting off any hard root pieces. Wash and chop roughly, setting one piece aside for proving the oil.

2. Remove the stalk from the red pepper and wash and chop roughly.

3. Place the tinned tomatoes, chopped onions, clove of garlic and chopped red pepper pieces into the jar of a blender/food processor and process to a fine paste. Add a little water/stock if necessary to aid the process and set aside.

4. Add oil to a medium-sized saucepan and heat on medium until a piece of onion added to the pan sizzles.

5. Add the blended onion mixture, tomato puree and spice mix to the pan and stir-fry on high heat until well mixed and the mixture begins to brown.

6. Add half the stock to the mix in the saucepan, then turn down the heat and simmer on low for 15-20 minutes until the oil rises to the top and it's cooked through

7. Add the steamed chicken pieces and heat through. If the sauce is too thick, add a little more stock until you have a thick, curry-like consistency.

8. Season to taste with salt and chilli sauce.

9. Serve hot with rice and side salad, mixed vegetables or boiled yams.

Several times Nain Jean experienced Naija stew in our house and round our Christmas table. I am convinced I influenced her palate, but she ate only a tablespoon of rice or stew.

On her eighty-first birthday my son and I took a tiny birthday cake to Nain Jean's house and celebrated her with hugs, kisses and laughs. That same year she called me into her spare room and handed me five vintage skirts, all in the same style but a different pattern, along with other odds and ends she said she was clearing out. Later that year my dear Nain Jean went to rest and left me with nothing to do on Tuesdays at 11am. But she left me with such delightful stories and memories that every time I think of her I just want to howl with laughter and order four chips and a slice of bacon.

I hardly go back to any of the cafes where we used to hang out, but the whole village and the surrounding area was aware of her passing and they often laugh over fond shared memories.

9. Dosbarth Cymraeg

Treiggladdau is the Welsh word for mutations, and these were the stumbling block for most of the people that I attended Welsh language classes and summer schools with over two years. Argh! You could pull your hair out! It didn't seem to make sense that the same word could start with a different letter depending on how it was used in a sentence, for example: *Penygroes pentre bach o Gymru, Dwi'n byw ym Mhenygroes, Dwi'n dod o Benygroes, Penygroes pentre bach o Gymru.* 'I live in Penygroes', 'I come from Penygroes', 'Penygroes is a small village in Wales' is the translation of the three previous statements. As I am writing this I am tickled, recalling the confusion and the frustration this used to cause in class.

They say you don't know what you don't know, so the first I knew about Welsh language classes for adults was the part-time ones that were run in my village and the next village by the school of life-long learning, Ysgol Gydol Oes. Totally unaware that there was any other way and in my enthusiasm to learn I immediately signed up to part-time classes and was on my way to becoming a Welsh speaker.

I was at home full time, being available for the children before and after school, and as a result I could organise my classes and my revision around their needs and timetables. Much later I found that there were immersion classes for adults which were held five days a week over three and six months, which would have been so much better for me, but by then life had already settled into a routine that made it impossible for me to attend those.

I loved learning Welsh, however, at a rate of two hours twice a week it was slow going. I would use Welsh at every opportunity: I attended every class and summer school that I could afford to, listened to radio shows, watched S4C, the Welsh TV channel, and engaged in telling my story using my limited knowledge of the language on TV cooking shows like the Welsh version of *Come Dine with Me* and with Chef Dudley.

Even now I don't like to watch replays of myself interviewing in Welsh and gesticulating while rolling my eyes like an emoji and trying to translate the next answer I need to give from English to Welsh. I am told this is not the best way to learn a language.

I enjoyed the process of learning when I had the leisure to do so, and the dreaded mutations made sense to me and my tongue, therefore I seemed to progress much quicker than others. When I first enrolled for Welsh classes, I did it with my friend Christine, who dropped out after two terms, finding the mutations too difficult and frustrating.

I started at the Ganolfan Talysarn with the lovely Helen Treharne, attended Bangor University life-long learning classes with the brilliant Elwyn Hughes, had Mark teach me in classes at Trigonos in Nantlle village, attended evening classes in the local senior school with Bronwen for a while and attended summer school at Bangor University. I was a good student, doing all my homework, and when The Melting Pot café was running it was a great opportunity to practise and listen to the language.

Elwyn Hughes is the author of the lifelong learning Welsh language courses and they were written with touches of humour that made it easier to remember. I recall that there was some laughter in Helen's classes and I learnt a lot, but there was so much mischief and laughter when Mark taught the classes that I learnt so many words and phrases that were not necessarily a part of the course book.

I met Nain Jean's older sister once on one of our many café-hopping trips and she asked if I had learnt the language. She wanted to know what swear words I had learnt, as this was really proof that I had integrated into the community, but, alas, neither Helen nor Mark taught these. She considered me not properly educated in the Welsh language as a result and promised to teach me the important words. That was the last time I saw her, so to date I have still not learnt the essence of the Welsh language.

Learning Welsh was so important to me at the time that when I attended the interview for the position of chef at the then Airport café, I explained that I needed to be free to attend my two-hour Welsh classes twice a week and that I could only work during school hours.

Like learning Welsh, the experience that is *garri* and *ekpa* or *garri* and groundnuts is something we learnt in boarding school and was a great, cheap go-to snack for those times toward the end of term when most of the goodies in our tuck boxes were gone.

Garri is the granular flour obtained by processing the starchy tuberous roots of cassava. In the Hausa language the term *garri* can be used to describe other granules obtained from other tubers or grains: *garin alkama* and *garin masara* are produced from maize, while *garin dawa* is the result from processing guinea corn that is made into a type of custard.

Cassava tubers are harvested, peeled, washed and grated or crushed to produce a mash which is then left to ferment. I remember using a locally crafted grater to do the job of grating cassava on several occasions for other cassava-based dishes.

The fermented grated mash is placed in a porous bag, which is then placed in an adjustable press machine for between one and three hours to remove excess water and dried.

Once dried, the mash is sieved and fried, with or without palm oil. The palm oil results in yellow *garri*, but the most popular is white Ijebu *garri*, which can be drunk like a porridge.

The resulting dry, granular *garri* can be stored for long periods and may be pounded or ground to make a fine flour. *Garri* is then enjoyed by mixing with boiling hot water to make a staple called *eba*, or, on a very hot day, mixed with ice-cold water and sugar, topped with *ekpa* or groundnuts and enjoyed as 'drinking *garri*'.

Several variations to this theme were developed in boarding school which you may want to experiment with including, adding a tablespoon or two of powdered milk, adding a spoonful of chocolate Milo, replacing the sugar with salt (we thought this was an adult version, urgh), adding sweetened condensed milk or just replacing the water with cold milk.

When my son was under ten, drinking *garri* was his go-to snack – he certainly had the tongue for it more than anyone in the home. As this product is not native to Wales, we would either have to buy it from ethnic shops in London when we visited, but for the more authentic Ijebu *garri* we would always bring a stash back with us any time we travelled to Nigeria or would ask visiting family to bring some. It is more readily found in ethnic shops all over Wales and the UK now.

Drinking Garri
1 part *garri*
3 parts cold water or milk
1 tablespoon sugar, to taste
A handful of peeled, roasted peanuts
(Nigerian: *ekpa*)

It is very important to note that *garri* swells a lot on the addition of a liquid, so start with a small portion.

Method

1. Soak the *garri* with the water or milk and allow to stand for about 30 seconds to one minute to soften.

2. Add the sugar and throw in a handful of roasted, peeled peanuts, or *ekpa*, and enjoy using a spoon.

I started my Welsh classes with the basic *cwrs wlpan*, the beginners' course, then on to *cwrs pellach* (intermediate) and went up to *cwrs uwch* (advanced), which I never managed to complete. I took the Mynediad (entry level) and Sylfaen (foundation) exams, including an oral test, but life and work meant that I stopped being able to attend formal classes and started to use my spoken Welsh at festivals and fairs when selling my products. Nostalgically, I still have the course books on my shelf as a reminder.

Very often at festivals and fairs there are still people who will speak only Welsh with me, and I feel so rusty and self-conscious compared to my previously confident Welsh speaking. I would really love to do an immersion course so I can be fully fluent.

10. Untying Women's Hands

When someone is unable to act freely because something prevents it, this is defined by Miriam Webster's dictionary as the saying 'my hands are tied'.

I dreamed of writing a cookery book as a young girl and started writing many versions several times. In the introductory chapter of my first book I mentioned how I had been writing it for over eighteen years in my head. Even after putting pen to paper and completing the first manuscript it was another four years before I finally set in motion the steps that led toward the day when I first held a copy in my hand.

I realised my hands were tied by my belief that it was only a certain type of person who became an author and that it was a very difficult journey. I had read much about being rejected many times before ever getting one look from a publisher. I had begun the journey to find a publisher but found it too hard, and I was never able to see through the journey to self-publishing. I realised that my thoughts around writing and publishing were the things that prevented me from acting freely.

In 2010 and 2012 some unexpected and tragic events occurred in my family that took me down a path of great sorrow and heaviness and what one doctor defined as periods of low mood. It was at this time I had a deep sense and longing to complete my 100 Things book. I did not know or think about how it would get published, I just followed the deep desire and continued to write and modify my manuscript. In that time a chance meeting to visit a friend resulted in us discussing the many books he had published. When we were departing, he gave me several copies of his book along with a promise that if I completed my book and sent the manuscript to him, he would get it published for me. And so, less than a year from the time I decided to pursue my dream of writing, I held the first copy of *100 Things I Wish My Mother Had Told Me* in my hands.

Oh, the elation, the excitement! I went all around the village telling everyone I knew about my book and showing them. After over forty years dreaming, I was now a published author. The editing wasn't fantastic, and I didn't sell a thousand copies, but my hands were no longer tied, and I knew that I had the freedom and ability to write and publish a book with help, nonetheless.

It is this passion to help untie women's hands, whether their freedom to act is driven from within like mine was or from external pressures, that is the passion behind the journey from caterer to teacher to trainer and now a food producer at Maggie's African Twist. I wish to be able to communicate through my journey and my products and my experience that there is a way to have one's hands sufficiently untied that will enable the effective use of our gifts and talents for the fulfilment of dreams and the contribution to our communities and society.

This book retells the journey I have taken to the fulfilment of long and short-held dreams that have finally come about because someone somewhere helped me see what was in my hands and gave me a push and sometimes a shove in the direction of its fulfilment, that I now believe in the total freedom to act for me and others in spite of where we find ourselves.

I dreamt and wrote about owning a café in 1978, but because of my age and the country I lived in I couldn't see how it could happen. Well, in North Wales I found the freedom to act, and The Melting Pot café was born and ran for over four years, with financial help from Gwynedd council, my dad, my friends the Chukwus and some money I had put in a savings plan ten years previous that matured just when I needed it.

The fulfilment of the dream of running my own food production business followed, as inspired by the 1980s movie *Baby Boom*, with the launch of our first products in May 2016 at Gwyl Fwyd Caernarfon under the name Maggie's Exotic Foods, which latterly has been changed into Maggie's An African Twist To Your Everyday Dish, or Maggie's African Twist for short, with over fifteen product lines and counting, providing employment opportunities for local youth and a single mum who has a child with particular needs.

In between the café and the food production business the freedom to become a published author came and I slowly and in a daze of sadness embraced it and today have the International Gourmand award-winning cookbook *The Melting Pot*, as well as *African Twist*, published by Graffeg and selling in mainstream bookshops. This was the fulfilment of a dream supported by the Welsh Government.

I thought my hands were tied in several ways that would have prevented me from being able to travel the road I have and experienced my journey because at some points in life I had learnt that being black, female, Nigerian and other adjectives were a deterrent to fulfilling my big dreams.

Once I got a taste of freedom there was nothing I couldn't achieve if I dreamed it. Maggie's African Twist now serves you up amazing African inspired, creamy smooth and tasty chilli-based sauces, easy-to-use spice mixes that liven up any food without adding calories and additives, in fact, some of the herbs and spices used in their production have such positive health-giving benefits.

Zobo, a drink made from the sepals of the hibiscus plant and very popular in Nigeria, has great health benefits, being high in Vitamin C as well calcium, iron, magnesium, potassium and other vitamins and trace elements which are vital for the healthy development of the body. This was a drink that I grew up vaguely aware of but did not appreciate until I started researching deeper into African foods.

In Hausa, one of the three main languages spoken in Nigeria (there are more than five hundred dialects spoken in Nigeria, with English the medium through which school is taught and pidgin English the uniting language), the edible plant *Hibiscus sabdariffa* is known as *zobo*, and a drink made from its sepals. Though native to Africa, this plant is popular in Jamaica and other parts of the West Indies, where it is known as Roselle.

Often at our pop-up restaurants you would be welcomed with a variation of *zobo*, and at Christmas time with a mulled spiced version of this deeply scarlet drink, sweetened with sugar or honey and a touch of lemon.

Zobo
Ingredients
3 litres water
75g dried sorrel
1 tablespoon fresh ginger, grated
1 teaspoon allspice berries
½ teaspoon cloves
Lemon peel
Sugar, honey or syrup to sweeten

Method
1. Place the *zobo* leaves in a large saucepan and pour in 2.5 litres of water. (The pan should not smell or taste of any other cooking to avoid absorbing those flavours.)

2. Add in the grated ginger, lemon slice, allspice and cloves.

3. Place the lid on the saucepan, then bring the contents to the boil under high heat.

4. Reduce the heat and allow the contents to boil for 25 minutes.

5. Add sugar or other sweetener according to taste, stir well and leave to steep and cool overnight.

6. Pass through a very fine mesh or muslin cloth.

7. Chill in the fridge.

8. Serve garnished with a slice of lemon.

I have shared with you a melting pot flavoured with experiences that impacted the senses, increased the resolve, strengthened the mental and physical muscles and all have combined to make a delightful platter of a life.

As we approach the final stop, there is still a lot of life yet to be lived, birthing possibilities and fulfilling dreams in Wales, helping to untie hands in lives and communities.

The call became Y Grochan Blasus, then Maggie's Exotic Foods, and has settled at

Maggie's An African Twist To Your Everyday Dish. We think our name is now self-explanatory and wherever you meet me in or out of the context of food, you will experience everything I have to offer with an African twist.

I hope you have enjoyed this journey with me, and that you, like me after reading *Bread Alone*, are inspired to give these recipes a go and enjoy the journey of trying. I also wish that you are inspired enough by my story to continue yours, and if there are things, internal or external, that are keeping your hands tied, please realise that there is always a way to pursue a dream.

Glossary

Baghrir – A traditional Moroccan pancake.

Calabash (also known as igba in Yoruba or duma in Hausa) – A utensil made from the dried, hollowed out shell of a fruit in the Lagenaria siceraria family and used in Nigerian households.

Cwrs Pellach – An intermediate-level course for Welsh learners.

Cwrs Uwch – An advanced-level course for Welsh learners.

Cwrs Wlpan – An intensive Welsh language course for beginners.

Dodo (dohdoh) – Nigerian dish of sliced and fried plantains.

Efo riro – Nigerian spinach stew.

Ekpa – Nigerian word for peeled, roasted peanuts.

Esekeseke (Bakweri)/uhio (Igbo)/prekese – Names used for the plant species *Tetrapleura tetraptera*, commonly used as a spice for soups in Africa.

Ewa – Nigerian bean stew.

Foofoo, foufou, fufu, eba, sadza, nsima (nshima), ugali – Different names used for the dumpling-type dough served as a staple all over Africa.

Garri – The granular flour obtained by processing the starchy tuberous roots of cassava.

Hausa, Igbo, Yoruba – Some of the many languages spoken in Nigeria.

Kpomo – Smoked and dried cow skin, a celebrated part of Nigerian cuisine.

Nain – Welsh term for grandmother.

Naira – The currency of Nigeria.

Puff-puff – Nigerian term for a traditional dried dough snack.

Treiggladdau – The mutations which are part of Welsh grammar.

Tuwon shinkafa – A soft, sticky and thick pudding made from local rice and enjoyed in Nigeria.

Ysbyty – Hospital in Welsh.

Ysgol/ysgolion – School/schools in Welsh.

Zobo – A popular Nigerian drink made from the sepals of the hibiscus plant.

Quick Reads

Quick Reads offer a series of short, engaging books which appeal to all tastes and reading abilities for the price of £1 each, encouraging less confident readers to pick up a book. These titles are aimed at adults who find reading a struggle or who've lost the habit of reading, and are also perfect for readers who are short of time. The initiative is coordinated in Wales by the Books Council of Wales and supported by the Welsh Government.